THING, THINK
Helen Hawley

Thing, Think
Helen Hawley
Copyright © 2023 Helen Hawley
All rights reserved
ISBN 979-8-9878589-0-5
Paperback
First Edition
Poetry

Hawsley

Contents

Dry \\ /// Green	7	
Parking Lot		8
World, Gorge		9
An Object to an Orbit		11
Hindsight		12
Pastimes		13
Strikes in a Dictionary	14	
Sprinkler & Letter T		15
Yves Tanguy		16
Toothpaste	17	
Calling Cindy		18
Sliding Jaws		20
Hazards		21
Back to Back	22	
Muscle is to Mussel		23
Blank and Blanket		24
Wool	25	
True-life Drama		26
Mars Touches Venus	27	
Zero		28
Southbound	29	
Load		30
Line in Motion		31
Notes		33

Dry \\ /// Green

I like making the shape of the letter a,
bending legibility until *a* is *not-a*.
I'm not the only person into
typography so, Why do I feel lonely?
Online, I admire drawings,
the free lines of Ellsworth Kelly's
pine branches. And they remind
me of days I'd sit under a tree
sorting needles, dry \\ /// green.

Parking Lot

Talk to me in a low voice.
Tell me about someone
who loved you. Let's eat
in the parking lot, be plain.
Some peaks are nameless.

World, Gorge

Under a streetlight, I saw a jar on a bench
with a message scribbled on it.

*Why should you not speak to me?
And why should I not speak to you?*

These words went inside, baring
the gulf between us and the loneliness
splitting the world. Astonished,
I said to nobody, Who wrote this?
—Whitman

Since the pandemic, silence is a fortress.
We all need someone to talk to
but who *besides you* listens?

At least the dead can speak
and it's thrilling, anything,
anything, scratches my living heart.

o

An Object to an Orbit

I remember when Jupiter and Saturn
saved each other from a fiery death.
You and I were together then
—two plumes of Pompeian red.
At sea, I saw you in every direction.
Time passed and we grew smaller.
Night by night the sky widens.

Hindsight

A poem that ends with a question
turns around to ask, What am I doing?

I end my days with a question.
What have I done?

Pastimes

I moved off road again. Behind the shed
is a small pond. The road's not maintained
by the county. Your city apartment sits
empty.

Navigating wide territories takes
sky instruments. Radio waves can relay
messages far as galactic space.

<<I signal>>
<<radio silence>>

While you travel narrow channels of a canal inland,
on another continent, my head swims.

Strikes in a Dictionary

Bye, **automobilize**. Bye, **aberglaube**:
belief in the unverifiable and unseen.

For the last time in print? I photographed it
—wisp, a flyaway. I'm not superstitious
but in myths, winds are fated.

To talk to a spirit you'll need a candle,
the lecturer said. So I took notes
in case I needed to talk later.

Alive or dead, we flock to a flickering light.
By this light, we've been writing and drawing
for more than thirty-thousand years.

Some words are so perfectly arranged
you wonder, Has enough been said?
Cuneiform to text message—we're not done yet.
Sleep fell over his eyes like wool
is the first recorded metaphor.

Sprinkler & Letter T

t-uh t-uh t-uh t-uh t-uh

t-uh t-uh t-uh t-uh t-uh

Yves Tanguy

Yves, you rhyme with yourself.
Now, what about genealogies? Not by birth,
but similarity to Miró, Noguchi and Bosch.
To be related, what a thrill. How I *feel*
looking at your gummy pinks. You seem
familiar with dentistry. Yves Tanguy,
you paint sand-crawling extractions.
Members of your encampments appear
twisted, bent or dented. In a wasteland,
what can be mended? Or resurrected?
You remind me that categories
like *old* and *new* are collapsing
volumes.

Toothpaste

The toothpaste has been emptied
into the sink. You sure squeezed it.
I stare at the glutinous squirt,
another mean delivery. Stop it,
would you? Stop disturbing the peace.

Calling Cindy

Hello.
Hello, is Cindy there?
No.
This isn't Cindy?
It isn't.
Do you ...
know anyone named Cindy?

Mail forwarded by the tenant
who moved into my old apartment
was annotated: Helen ≠ Tom

Hold on Tom, Can I call you
Larry? Is it for sure I am not you
and Cindy isn't me?

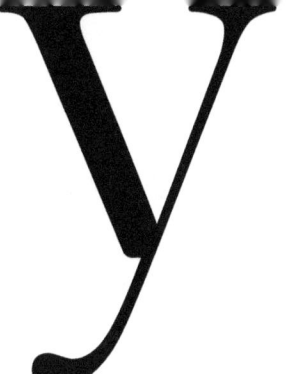

Sliding Jaws

For sliding jaws,
words are chewy.
The more right
the words, the more
real they feel.

Hazards

When the ice melts, the deck
gets slippery, slippery as film
over my eyes in the morning,
hazardous as word-finding
in my hurting head.
        Another slip
keeps me away from you.
As we skate apart, I throw coarse salt.
You describe the salt as *biting*.
When the ice melts, it's all too slick.

Back to Back

I dig and you fill.
I dig and you fill.
—*You*, dig. I'll fill.
You dig and I fill.
I dig and I fill.

Alternate titles generated by GPT-3: 1. A Tale of Digging and Filling 2. Gilgamesh's Laborious Journey: The Digging and Filling Saga 3. Gilgamesh's Toil: A Poem of Digging and Filling 4. The Epic of Gilgamesh: A Story of Backbreaking Work 5. Gilgamesh's Burden: The Digging and Filling Odyssey 6. A Poem of Unending Drudgery

Muscle is to Mussel

Muscle is sometimes confused with *mussel*.

Muscle is to *hard*, as *mussel* is to *juicy*.
Muscle is to *flexing*, as *mussel* is to *sh*ucking.

Blank and Blanket

A blanket of snow
covers the ground.
I stow a blanket
for emergencies.
Windburned and
snowblind. I don't mind
the cold blasting
blank after blank
clear through me.

Wool

HAND WASH - COLD
NO WRING OR TWIST
BLOCK TO DRY FLAT
DO NOT BLEACH

True-life Drama

Something wet and cold climbs into bed. You inch backward as it creeps forward.

Your hair! you exclaim.

Warm me, I smile.

You are not dry.

Don't turn away (I'll cry).

Mars Touches Venus

Mars wears a gleaming helmet
in the richly colored bedroom
where the goddess sits. Her eyes
meet ours over her shoulder.
We follow Mars' arm and feel
what he feels with our eyes.

Zero

I google the difference
between a number and a numeral,
the difference
between zero and none.
Zero has limits, none hasn't.
A null set is empty.
In the woods, years pass
uneventfully, but one night
the moon, a dime
in the sky, is eclipsed
by a black disc—
What's my size?

Southbound

Ride into the countryside.
Take in your arms (soil).
Take in your arms
the people who love you.

Load

a pencil, one lead, two lead.
Fill a basket, one bread, two bread.
We used to sleep in, one bed.

Line in Motion

Longer than wide,
a line is theoretically endless.
Practically, it's the shortest
distance between us. Lines crest,
trough, break, lie slack or straight.
I say, *Writing is a system of organized lines*,
when I'm teaching. *To make a drawing,
put a line in motion*. It sounds easy.
I am given *a line*. Lines are implied,
crossed, crossed out and underlined.
I wait in line. Wait for directions.
Impatient for momentum, I plan the next
exhibition. Twist cherry veneer
into a Mobius strip. On the path
of this line, I'll never *arrive*.

Notes

I started writing these poems during the pandemic, the winter of 2021. Thank you, Chele and John, for the sanctuary.

The font is Cardillac, designed by Dieter Hofrichter.

The Oakland Review first published *Yves Tanguy.*

La Piccioletta Barca, UK, first published *An Object to an Orbit.*

Eunoia Review, Singapore, first published *Pastimes and Parking Lot.*

Striking A Word was inspired by a NYT article: 'Aberglaube' was expunged from a supplement of the OED and later reinstated. Kaufman, Leslie. "Dictionary Dust-Up (Danchi is Involved)" New York Times, Nov 29, 2012. The first use of metaphor is often attributed to *Gilgamesh*, as mentioned in the BBC: In Our Time podcast hosted by Melvyn Bragg in the episode: History of Metaphor.

Tofu Ink Arts Press first published *Mars Touches Venus.* I based this poem on a painting by Lavinia Fontana: *Mars and Venus*, c. 1595. In the last line, I paraphrase the 1958 film, *The Horses Mouth*. The character, Gully Jimson, explains, "I'll show you how to understand a painting. Don't look at it. Feel it with your eyes."

Photo: Abdou Aziz

Helen Hawley is a visual artist and poet from Missouri. She attended the Rhode Island School of Design and the University of Wisconsin in Madison. She has taught drawing and painting at Beloit College and the University of Wisconsin. Her art has been shown in Chicago, New York, and Beijing. This is her first chapbook of poetry.

www.ingramcontent.com/pod-product-compliance
Lightning Source LLC
Chambersburg PA
CBHW032109040426
42449CB00007B/1227